I0017143

BEGINNERS GUIDE TO ARDUINO:

A COMPLETE GUIDE ON EVERYTHING YOU NEED TO KNOW ABOUT ARDUINO

By

Ken Edward

Copyright 2020, Ken Edward

CONTENTS

INTRODUCTION

WHAT IS ARDUINO?

Arduino is an easy-to-use electronic platform or board that is based upon an open source software and hardware program. It was created in Italy at the Ivrea Interaction Design Institute, following the need to have a tool which can be used for quick prototyping.

The Arduino Company is a manufacturer of microcontroller kits and single-board microcontrollers which are used for constructing digital devices. The prototyping ability of this device is because it has been furnished with pins which can be interfaced with other expansions on the Arduino boards.

Although, programming and electronics may sound difficult for some people, Arduino in its early years of development was majorly made for people who have no background knowledge in programming and electronics. Now, nearly any person with or without the required programming and electronics skill, can use this unique tool. Hackers, hobbyists, designers, artists, newbies and any other person can make use of the Arduino for various purposes that specifically suit their aim.

The two main parts of the Arduino are its software or Integrated Development Environment (IDE) and physical software (the microcontroller) which are licensed by GNU Lesser General Public License (LGPL) and CC-BY-SA respectively.

The continuous improvement and development that the Arduino board has undergone now make it useful for various difficult day-to-day activities. This is because it has been uniquely differentiated from the simpler 8-bit boards. Now, it is a product used for IoT applications, 3D printing, embedded environments and wearable. Arduino is capable of interacting with GPS units, the internet, LEDs, motors, speakers, cameras, TVs and even your mobile smart phones.

The Arduino is created mainly for anyone who has the passion for creating an interactive environment or object. This may range from creating an honest fortune-telling machine to a heating pad hand warming blanket. Just almost anything that can be created.

Many Arduino boards are typically made up of an Atmel 8-bit AVR microcontroller. Other things that are on these Arduino boards are the pins, flashy memory and several other features. Connections for programming and incorporation into many other circuits are facilitated by the use of double row or single pins.

Why is Arduino popular?

The popularity of Arduino is generally increasing among users all over the world. This can be attributed to many factors and exclusive features of this device. Some of the reasons why people prefer the device include (but not limited to) the followings

- **The ease of use:** Because many people are starters when it comes to electronics, they prefer the Arduino since it does not require any additional piece of hardware (or programming) before a new code can be loaded onto the board.
- **Easy installation:** Arduino is very easy to install. This is because it has its own distinctive USB chip. With this unique USB chip, the installation of the Arduino software becomes a lot easier.
- **Simple programming language:** In addition to this, the Arduino IDE uses the simple form of one of the easiest programming language (the C and C++). This makes its usage and accessibility better.
- **Relatively cheaper access:** Arduino Company made their software free and the hardware is relatively cheap, hence, many of its users find it easy to contribute their own knowledge such as

coding and other instructions for many of the Arduino-based projects.

- **Good back-up:** Almost all electronic devices can be backed up by the Arduino. In fact, some models of this device are used to load programs from personal computers. This is done by using the standard API known as "Arduino language".

- **Replaceable processor:** Arduino has a processor which can be quickly replaced as soon as any impairment is detected. This makes it a better device when it comes to replaceable parts.

- **Speed of communication:** Many users of Arduino like it because of its speed. Arduino has a fast communication speed with a personal computer. This ensures easy transfer of information between Arduino and any PC.

If you are wondering where you might be able to get this device, the Arduino products are available from the official website of the company and from other distributors that have been authorized.

CHAPTER ONE

WHY IS IT ADVANTAGEOUS TO USE ARDUINO?

Arduino has several excellent features which make it preferred for many people especially for beginners who usually see it as a tool which can be used to control much electronic devices. Some of the merits of Arduino include

- **Boot loader makes loading programs easy:** Arduino can be used to load programs directly without burning the program on the device by hardware programmers. This is because of its boot loader which dumps programs on the circuit.

- **Cheaper cost:** Arduino can be gotten for a far lesser price when compared to other similar devices. Most development boards cost $50 upwards in the market. Arduino can be bought at a price of around $30 without any compromise when it comes to its.

- **IDE:** Arduino has an IDE which is capable of running on Windows, Linux or Macs. This is because it has been manufactured based on an open source tool and a durable and well-supported backend. This makes it better for porting. Aside from this, it is easier to find bugs and fix them.

- **Strong IDE community:** Many users of the Arduino enhance the quality of its IDE by working tirelessly and improving on it. This can be majorly be attributed to the quality and affordability of the Arduino.

- **Simple design:** Many boards which have been developed and are similar to Arduino come with a complex design. In such boards, many multifaceted structures like LEDs, buttons, LCD and several other segments comes along with it. This makes such boards to be bulky.

Arduino has been developed with a very simple and modest structure. This is because there are several Arduino shields (ranging from Wi-Fi to LCD) that users can add or not add to Arduino based on the function they want it to perform.

- **Arduino Libraries perform several functions:** Arduino has been made with Libraries which can perform several tasks. These tasks can range from complex function such as parsing GPS or writing to SD cards to simple things such as debounce buttons or twiddle pins.

- **Arduino is to a product of a Chip Maker:** Many Chip makers usually want to make their own products to be unique. This makes them to manufacture Chips which have parts that will set them apart from other manufacturers of similar chips.

Arduino, however, is not a product of any Chip maker. Hence it has been purposefully designed to exhibit similarities between many microcontrollers. This means that whatever can be done on any microcontroller can also be done on the Arduino.

- **Sensors:** Arduino has an analog-to-digital input which makes it a good digital sensor. Arduino will measure temperature and light intensity using data that has been provided by the sensor. Nearly all sensors that can be found in the market can be used in this case.

- **Arduino is light and runs on a metal:** The Arduino code has a good and intelligent compiler which runs straight on a bare metal. Even with this, it is very light, fast and small. The codes are not actually interpreted like the BASIC or NET but it comes along with the HEX which may be used to in bulks to program fresh chips.

Disadvantages of Arduino

- **Small resolution:** The resolution of the Arduino microcontroller is just 10 bit. Hence, if you need a better working memory or processing power which may arise as a result of increase in function of the device, Arduino may not be a very good option because it cannot handle compound and advanced functions.

- **No debugger:** No debugger comes along withthe Arduino. Hence, you may not be able to check scripts. Once you cannot track your progress and operations, it becomes difficult for you to detect any error that might have occurred.

- **Limited program execution:** Arduino can only execute a minute number of programs at the same time. This may be especially frustrating if you are a type that likes to multi-task your device. Its usage has therefore been limited to micro-equipment, hence, you cannot multi-task on the Arduino.

- **No knowledge of AVR microcontroller:** Beginner who uses Arduino may find it difficult to understand the AVR microcontroller. This particularly affects the overall efficiency in operating the device.

- **Its programming language:** Arduino mainly make use of the C and C++ programming languages. These programing languages are, however, better understood by experienced programmers and not just some newbie.

- **Small RAM and memory:** Arduino can never be substituted for your own PC. Therefore, the things that can be done and stored on it are always limited. Arduino has just 2 kilobyte of RAM and 32 kilobyte of flash memory.

- **It is not an all fix board:** Although, the Arduino can operate various other devices and can as well be used as PC accessory but it is not a fix-all device as it is not adequately optimized for such general function

- **No partitioning of code:** Arduino does not have a good project environment because of the IDE used. This makes no room for other files and does not even encourage easy learning. Many of the users just go online and copy codes without a good understanding of what they are doing.

- **Usage of 5V:** Many Arduinos still make use of the 5V instead of the 3.3V which offers the best when it comes to speed and accuracy. This is an old fashion way because the older chips are slower and their 5V is too low.

- **Misuse of Arduino:** Many users of Arduino use it for some task which is really not necessary. This is because they generally lack deep understanding of how it works and they see the device as an easy fix to almost anything they want to do.

- **Abstracted API:** Arduino has not-too-sure API. These abstracted APIs are latent. Because of this, the normal interaction between several applications is hindered. Hence, there little or no data transfer between the components involved.

- **Port manipulation:** This is another great disadvantage posed by the Arduino. Most users go ahead to manipulate the device's port instead of pins. This is because of the lack of knowledge of basic programming language. Most users do not know that an equivalent of the C exist within the Arduino which can be used to change such manipulations.

CHAPTER TWO

ARDUINO BOARDS (TYPES)

Types of Arduino Boards and Its Uses

Arduino boards have been used to design various engineering projects. Some embedded engineers sometimes use it as a finishing touch for their projects. These designs varies, ranging from a complex scientific instrument to something as a simple as a domestic or household instrument.

All of these Arduino boards are open-source. This has enhanced its ability to be used for several different applications. There are different types of Arduino boards with varied as well as similar features which are sometimes based on the specific project they are used for. Some of the types of Arduino boards are

- **Arduino Leonardo Board**: The Leonardo board came as one of the first developments of Arduino boards. This board can directly use USB making it easier for the usage of program libraries. The USB being used come along with one microcontroller making it a cheap and easy to use board.

  This feature of the Leonardo boards makes it to be used along with the computer keyboard, mouse etc. The board has a processor called ATmega32u4 with a speed of 16 MHz. The SRAM memory is 2.5 KB while the flash memory is 32 KB.

- **Arduino Uno (R3)**: The Arduino Uno is one of the most popular Arduino boards used by people of varied professions. The digital input/output (I/O) comprises of 14 pins out of which6are utilized as a PWM output (i.e. pulse width modulation). Some other things found in this board are a USB connection, a reset button, a power jack and 6-analllog input.

All these are able to be used to uphold the microcontroller. This board can be attached to your PC using a USB cable. The board has a processor called ATmega328 with a speed of 16 MHz. The SRAM memory is 2 KB while the flash memory is 32 KB.

- **RedBoard Arduino Board:** The RedBoard Arduino board uses the Arduino IDE. This Arduino IDE is subsequently programmed by the usage of a Mini-B USB cable. This easily functions well with Windows 8 and there will be no need to adjust any of your security settings.

  The RedBoard Arduino board can be easily controlled. When it has been eventually created, it is one of the easiest to use. Just select from the menu option after you might have plugged the board.

- **LilyPad Arduino Board:** This board is a sort of e-textile technology that is wearable. They are specially designed for textiles and they can also be washed. They are made in such a way that the threads are used from them to sew them into clothing. Their sensor boards, power and I/O are also specifically designed for this purpose. This board also consists of an Arduino bootloader and Atmega with 2V to 5V power supply.

- **Arduino Mega (R3)**: The Arduino Mega has an ATmega2560 processor and its digital I/O pins are 54. Four of these pins are used for the serial port of the UART hardware, sixteen of them for analog inputs and fourteen are utilized as the output for PWM. Some other compositions of this boards are a power jack, connection for USB, ICSP header, RESET pin and the 16 MHz crystal oscillator.

- **Arduino Shields**: The Arduino shields are usually used to connect to other types of Arduino boards. They pre-built circuit boards. These Arduino shield also varied based on the type of usage. Some of these Shields include Proto Shield, Ethernet Shield, Wireless Shield and GSM Shield.

The Arduino boards and Arduino Shield are connected in such a way that the Arduino board is coupled under the Arduino Shield. This facilitates easy communication as the board is eventually connected to control the LCD and monitor.

- **Arduino Micro Boards:** This is another special type of Arduino board which has a very small design. The microcontroller has a processor dubbed ATmega32U4. Out of the 20 pins that it contains, 12 are used for analog I/O and 7 are for PWM. The micro-USB connection is not separated but comes along with the Arduino Micro board.

  Aside from this, other notable features of the board include an ICSP header, a crystal oscillator of 16 MHz. Because the Arduino micro is small and resembles the Arduino Leonardo boards, it is usually said to be a shrunk kind of the Leonardo.

- **Arduino Due Board**: The Arduino Due is the first set of Arduino board that has been designed to be based on the ARM microcontroller. The ARM core is 32-bit and out of the 54 digital I/O pins it contains, 12 are analog pins. There are two different types of ports on this board (the programming port and the USB port). The programming port serves as the attachment point for the micro side of the USB cable.

- **Arduino Bluetooth Board:** The Arduino BT boards are microcontrollers with the processor ATmega168. It has been specifically termed as a Bluetooth board because its programming can occur via a wireless connection of Bluetooth. The other features of this board are screw terminals, crystal oscillator of 16 MHz, reset button, 6 analog pins and 16 digital pins.

- **Arduino Explorer Board:** The Arduino Explorer board has been specially designed for actuators and sensors to easily interface. The other main features that make this board different from other types of Arduino boards are its microphone, joystick, temperature sensor, accelerometer, slider and buttons. On the Arduino Explorer board is the input and output connection.

What Arduino board can be useful in the house?

Several types of the Arduino boards can be used at home for various purposes. Although the function which such Arduino will perform will give insight into which type of board to use, but the Arduino Uno, Arduino Mega, Arduino Pro and Arduino Mini have been the most used Arduino boards in many homes.

This is because the major functions they are being used for at home ranges from scheduling upcoming events and switching on or off the lights to even operating your smartphones. The Arduino Uno particularly offers the best quality especially for beginners.

CHAPTER THREE

HOW TO CONNECT YOUR ARDUINO TO A COMPUTER

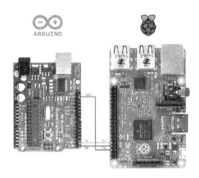

After being sure of the type of Arduino board you will use for any specific function. The next thing to do is to try and load the set of program or codes into the Arduino board via a computer. It is based on these loaded programs that your Arduino will function. This programs or set of codes are, however, very precise to the function they will perform.

Whatever instructions passed into the Arduino board is what will get executed. To load your codes on the Arduino, it must be connected to your computer. The following are the things you will need to establish the required connection

- The Arduino board
- The Arduino software
- The USB cable (A and B plug)
- Your computer

1. Start by downloading the software compatible with your Arduino.
2. Once this has been done, you can unzip it (D:/Arduino).
3. Then, establish a connection between your computer and Arduino board by connecting the USB port on your computer while the other end of the USB cable is connected to your Arduino board.
4. When your computer's Windows request for the driver, you can manually install it (location is D:/Arduino/arduino-0022/drivers).
5. The Arduino software environment can then be found at D:/Arduino/arduino-0022/arduino.exe.

6. After this, you can now choose the type of Arduino board you are using by doing the following
- Go to Tools
- Select board
- Then, choose the type of Arduino board from the lists of drop-down options
7. Choose the serial port by going to Tools, serial port then COM
8. Go to sketch example by choosing Fire, Examples, Basics and Blink
9. Upload the code to Arduino by clicking on the upload button. When you see that the "Done uploading" prompt as appeared, your Arduino has been installed successfully.

Establishing a connection of Arduino to your computer

Tool required by Arduino for easy connection

After you might have successfully installed your running code on the Arduino board. The next thing is how to execute the specific project.

Several of the projects that an Arduino can do may range from flying a drone, lightening a LED or moving a simple robot to locking a door (Some of the project you can try with Arduino are discussed later).

If any of these projects are to be executed, there is need to upload the specific program or set of codes on your Arduino board (this can be seen from the above on how to connect your Arduino to a computer). These codes are particular to the very function that such an Arduino is going to perform.

After this might have been done, the next thing is to painstakingly connect every other component parts of the Arduino to the device you want it to function with. This is done using some simple tools or instruments. Some of the working tools that are needed for any Arduino project include

- **Wire strippers:** These are plier-like portable tools. They are usually held in the hand and used to remove the outer covering of any electrical wire. They can as well be used to cut open any end on an electrical wire. Such ends are often connected to the end of another opened wire.

For the Arduino project, this tool is used to make a connection of wires from your Arduino to the instrument you are working with. This allows the transfer of useful information that is specific to the basic function of that project

- **Precision screw driver set:** These set of screw drivers are usually used by many technicians or hobbyist. They are made in set with different slots that can be changes for any particular screw.

  Because of the intricate nature of your Arduino board, these precision screw drivers are often needed especially for minute or small screwing. In this way, these drivers can grip and at the same time twist on the necessary small portions/instruments of the project you are doing.

- **Needle-nose pliers:** Needle-nose pliers have several names. Some of the names this tool is popularly called include snipe-nose plier, pointy-nose plier, pinch-nose plier and log-nose plier. It is both a holding and cutting tool especially for the several intricate wires that comes along with the Arduino project.

These tools are used mainly for snipping, bending or repositioning any wire in you Arduino project so that it will be well placed and as such gives the Arduino the optimum function you want. This is because they are able to get to a very tight position where other regular pliers may not be able to function.

- **Flush Cutters:** This tool is popularly used to cut your wires. Using flush cutters allow the place where such wires are cut to be neat, flat and very smooth. Flush cutters are held in a position which is perpendicular to any wire you may want to cut. Using this cutter in your Arduino project makes your work absolutely neat and perfect.

- **Digital Multimeter:** A multimeter will generally measure the values of electricity passing through your device. Majorly, most digital multimeter will measure values in volts (V), amps

(A) and ohms (Ω). This tool will measure those parameters with good accuracy. You will get to know the values of either the current, voltage or resistance of electricity passing through your device so as to make any necessary adjustment if the need arise

- **Fine tip straight tweezers:** This tool is used to pick up any remains of unnecessary debris or materials that has find its way into your project. It has two ends; one is a pointed end used specifically for the tweezing purpose while the other end is a picking end.

- **Solder sucker:** This is a desoldering instrument popularly known as a desoldering pump. It is mainly used to remove any previously soldered part of your device. This might majorly be for repair, replacement or troubleshooting of that part.

- **Soldering iron:** The soldering iron is a tool used to connect the various wires within your project. This ensures the transfer of electric charges across the whole component of the project. It is often heated and then used to melt the solder. The solder glues the necessary components part you wish to join together.

- **Panavise Jr:** A Panavise Jr is another tool that is important for Arduino project. This tool is used to hold any part of your project for easy assortment. It can hold your Arduino board, or accompanying part of the board.

Doing this makes it easier for you to do anything you want to do on your project because this tool can eventually be twisted to any position you want offering you the desired comfort that comes along with doing your project.

Careful precautions should be taken when connecting every component part of your device with your Arduino board to avoid the problem of incorrect connection and to also avoid tampering with any other part which may necessarily not be need currently for the project you are doing.

Preparation work before your project is finally done

Once the required code for the particular device or function has been created and uploaded to your Arduino. You just need to connect the necessary part of your Arduino with the specific device it will function on using some tools (many of which has been described above).

After this has been done, you will now need to ensure that all the necessary connection is correctly put in place and there is no mistake whatsoever. First, ensure that the running code is the right code for the project. Ensure that all necessary tools and/or devices are placed correctly to avoid wrong combination of connection.

This is a very important step because any mistake done will undermine the entire purpose of the process. After being sure that all necessary connections are correct, it is now time to let our device perform its function.

Testing your connection

After ensuring that all what has been done is right, starting from the uploading of the code to the general assembling of various components of the project and giving it a finishing touch. The next thing is to see whether or not the project will function. This can simply be done by just executing the project.

For instance, if your project is based on putting on or off a LED light, just press on the switch and see if the LED light will be on or off or if your project is based on a finger print door, just put your fingerprint on your project and see if the door will open (more on the possible projects you can try using your Arduino later).

If the LED light turns on/off when you press the switch or the fingerprint door open at the prompt of your fingerprint, then your project has been perfectly executed. If not, it probably means that the code being run is wrong or the connections done are not right. This will warrant further troubleshooting.

CHAPTER FOUR

THE ARDUINO MEGA SERVER

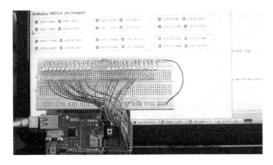

The Arduino Mega Server serves as the operating

system for your Arduino. Users have been at advantage of using this server because of its ease of use. It also supports some web functions, hardware and network functions. Using the Arduino Mega server enables you to be able to surf the internet and do any other things online. This has been made possible because of its dynamic user interface and good graphics.

This Mega server is often used with an Arduino Ethernet Shield and a micro SD card. These unique set functions together to achieve a smooth use of the web. The Ethernet Shield particularly brings out the role of the Arduino Mega Server. This makes sure that you access the server via your computer. By doing this, you will be able to connect any browser on your computer to the same network being used by your Arduino. This also makes sure that you are able to

- Use Javascripts from webpages to control hardware
- Use simple HTML to read a switch state
- Use HTML to read a sensor's value

If you have been considering using your Arduino for surfing the internet, the followings are the things you will need.

- An Arduino Mega Server (e.g. Arduino Mega2560 or Arduino UNO)
- A wired LAN connection having a speed of 10/100MB

- An Ethernet Shield

  The major function of the Ethernet Shield is to connect to the internet using the Arduino as the source of connection. Your Arduino is connected by putting the head pins of your shield into it. The Shield is then connected to an Ethernet cable. Other hardware that are required when doing this include

- Ethernet cable
- Pushbutton
- 9 V adaptor
- Wi-Fi router
- Jumper wires
- 10 K resistors
- Breadboard

  These tools are put in place to allow several optimal functions such as real time clock, integration with smart home systems, receiving and sending of certain commands from the network, searching for any available network, controlling of voltage and current, and maintenance of sensors and measurement of temperature.

Aside from this, you can also add any of your own personal modules that you want to add. This is because the Arduino Mega Server can selectively compile modules and detect the compiled modules, separating them from the modules that were not compiled. You also have the ability to either disable or enable any module that has been compiled directly from the internet.

An electric module which can also monitor the voltage going in and out of the Arduino is one of the things that have been implemented with the Arduino Mega server. Aside from this, this electric module also monitors the current. It can be found on the switch board and can easily verify the details of the electricity consumed. One other unique function this module also performs is that it can also track the presence of people.

An oscilloscope for the network has been one of the many additions. This oscilloscope serves to read the dynamic signals or oscillogram that occurs as a result of network traffic within your web in real time. A screensaver module is also available which is mainly used for displaying information on panels. This allows you to specifically choose the main information you need while discarding any other information.

The Arduino Mega Server also prevents system failure by implementing a very powerful frequency meter. There is also a 216 block indicator useful for 3D system status, this allows you to easily look over the entire arrangement of the system. If you want to use your Arduino as a web server, you must do the following things

- Use the Ethernet configuration for the Arduino
- Stipulate the address of the IP
- Give the Address of the MAC you are using
- Connect your Arduino to the available internet service (you can use a Wi-Fi router for this)
- Give the code required to run Arduino as a web server

- Connect your computer to the Arduino using a router

Because of the simplicity of the set-up, many users of the Arduino Mega Server can connect a SD card of up to 32 GB. By doing this, you can easily use this SD card to save different content and files from the web server.

The Arduino Mega Server can also be integrated with Majordomo. The Majordomo platform is like a home automation system. By integrating it with the Arduino, you will be able to send data to analyze it and also send any status you need to send. You can also get command control from over the network and store data.

The Arduino Mega Server has always been termed to be used as a "tandem mode". This means that the resources of the Majordomo server are being used to function in the Arduino Mega Server. The Majordomo can, however, work independently as its major purpose is not mainly for the tandem mode.

The Arduino Mega Server is a processor of 8-bit capacity. This is a contributory factor to its multifunctional nature and many other unique features. Additionally, you are able to host as many sites as possible when using your Arduino Mega server. You can even update contents without turning off your controller or pulling out the memory card.

Using the Arduino Mega Server allows several web pages to modify themselves to adjust the screen of your computer. This gives you the best experience you may need when browsing especially if you are surfing the internet is for information purpose.

CHAPTER FIVE

PROGRAMMING LANGUAGES THAT ARDUINO USE

The programming language that the Arduino uses is often referred to as the Arduino programming language or simply the Arduino language. The Arduino expose its users to an array of integrated libraries and a programming editor. This makes it easy to load and compile these programs into the board.

The Arduino programming languages being purportedly used are by many people especially as a downloadable online tool is the C/C++ programming languages. Because these programs are very simple, they are usually called sketches.

These sketches usually refer to any files of text that has been written in the Arduino language. If you will need to save and then upload these sketches to your Arduino board, you will need to use the extension ". ion". The Arduino programming language is made up of the following

- **Functions:** These allow you to have total control of your Arduino board. Functions allow you to do simple programming stuff such as analyzing characters or executing any mathematical operation.

  The sketch of the Arduino programming language has function which can either be setup () or loop () function. The setup () is used for execution every time you power up and reset your button. The loop () is now used to power off and rest the button. The function main () does not exist in the Arduino language. Other functions useful when handling

- **Digital input and output (I/O):** They aredigitalRead() which its parameter is a pin number, digitalWrite() which gives a digital output pin value that may be either high or low, pinMode() which input and output is set as pin, pulseIn() which reads pulse from digital signal from low to high and back from high to low again, shiftIn() which reads byte bit by bit, shiftOut() which writes byte bit by bit among others.

- **Analog input and output (I/O):** They include analogRead () which uses an analog pin to read values, analogReference() which uses the analog input in configuring the value range for inputs, analogWrite() which writes an analog value to a pin etc

- **Time function:** They include delay() which can pause or delay a program that has been specified as a parameter for few milliseconds, delayMicroseconds() which can pause a program that has been specified as a parameter for a few microseconds etc.

- **Math function**: These include abs() which specifies a number's absolute value, constrain() which limits a number to be within a specified range, cos() which indicates an angle's cosine, sq() which indicates a number's square, pow() which means the value of a number which has been raised to a specific power etc.

- **Constant and variables:** These are Arduino values which are very similar to those used in the C++ programming. They are mostly used in the conversion of type. They offer easy transfer of necessary data within the Arduino environment.

- **Structure:** This is the last portion of the Arduino programming language. Here, we can find small code elements like operators and others. This structure gives the Arduino a major lift in the eventual execution of any written code.

You are also able to use the Arduino programming language to import external libraries. These libraries contain codes that have been already written. This gives you the ease of working; otherwise, you can write your won code or download the required code you want directly from the internet.

Most times, C libraries may be used. This is very specific for the Arduino language. Such libraries of languages need to be installed via the Library Manager that is on the Arduino IDE. Some of the online downloadable Arduino languages are

ArduBlock: This programming language has been used specifically by most beginners. Instead of typing a code, the ArduBlock offers you the easy access to construct your own code. You will be able to select functions to your codes. It is especially good for visual learners.

Snap4Arduino: This is also a visual programming language like the ArduBlock. It is usually used in a drag and drop manner. Although, it is very similar to the ArduBlock, but it is specially designed for users who are now getting hold of the Arduino programming language. If you want to install this language, you will need "StandardFirmata" that has been already installed on your Arduino.

C#: This allows easy way for your Arduino to share information with your computer. When you use this programming language, you will be able to code in another language that is entirely different from that being used as sketch by your Arduino. The "CmdMesseger" will particularly help you in doing this.

This messenger can be run in either the Microsoft Visual Studio or any other third-party alternative you may have at hand. The C# language then makes way for smooth communication between your computer and Arduino.

Python: Although, the Arduino cannot specifically use codes that are built upon the python programming language. Ti is however, able to communicate in this language by using the serial input that is on your device. This can be done by downloading the pySerial. Because this programming language is very intuitive, it is often the basic of some other advanced programming languages.

The programming language of Arduino is overall enhanced by the Arduino software (the IDE). This IDE are built upon both the wiring IDE and processing IDE which are used with the Arduino environment. Most users however prefer to use the online version of this software. This online version is called the Arduino Web editor. This is a very good option especially when coding using the Arduino.

This allows you to store several of your data directly into clouds thereby offering easy accessibility for you at any time that you may want to need it. The online version of the Arduino software is also advantageous because it does not require any further update unlike the online version. However, the offline version can always be downloaded and used for other users who prefer it.

Working with the Arduino programming language using the IDE makes the communication easy as the IDE is easily integrated with many computer platforms such as Windows, Linux and MacOS.

CHAPTER SIX

THE ARDUINO INTEGRATED DEVELOPMENT ENVIRONMENT

The Arduino IDE is a software application that can be used across varied platforms such as the Linux Windows or MacOS. Its function is written in the language of C/C++. This software serves as the intermediary used for writing and uploading programs to the Arduino boards. Several other tools such as toolbar with buttons, code writing text editor etc. also comes with the software. Aside from the facts above, the software is open-source and is used on all Arduino boards

Like discussed earlier, sketches are set of programs that have been written using the Arduino software. The text editor is used to write these sketches. You get to verify and upload any program using the toolbar buttons. The toolbar also functions for opening of the serial monitor and creating, opening and saving of sketches.

Downloading and installing the Arduino IDE

If you are ready to start using your Arduino for any project of your choice, then, it may be time for you to install the Arduino IDE software. To do this, you will first download the software online from the Arduino website. After you are done with this, you will be able to run any program using this Arduino software IDE. To do this,

- Enter the Arduino website (https://www.arduino.cc/en/Main/Software) on your web browser
- Click on the link to download and go to the download page
- Select the "I Agree" button on the License agreement for the Arduino
- Click on the Windows link on the download page, this will download the Arduino software which is specifically for Windows
- Find the file that you just downloaded on your computer, the, extract the zipped file
- Copy this to an easy-to-recognize place on your computer
- After this, connect the computer with the Arduino by attaching your Arduino board to the computer
- Commence the Windows device Manager by clicking on the Windows Start menu button
- Right-click the menu of "Computer" and select "properties" from the lists of the drop-down menus
- Click on the link of "Device Manager"

- After this, the Device Manager will show "Arduino".
- Update the driver software by right-clicking on the "Arduino".
- A dialogue box will show, the, choose "Browse my computer for driver software" from the drop-down options
- After this select the "Browse" button
- The downloaded Arduino folder now have a Driver folder, Choose this Drivers folder. After this has been chosen, you can now click "Next"
- A dialogue box will come up, choose the "Install this driver software anyway"

  After few minutes, the installation of the driver will be completed. You will notice that another dialogue box will come up, just note the port that has been used to configure the Arduino. After this, you can set-up your Arduino software. To do this,

- Go to the folder that has just been downloaded

- The Arduino software can now be opened by double clicking on it.
- Be sure that you have chosen the right Arduino board and if not, change from the option as necessary
- Be sure also that the serial port that has been chosen is the right one, if not, change as necessary

After all this has been done, what remains is for us to test our installation whether it is working or not. You are able to see if the installation is good by loading the sketch into the Arduino. To do this, Select the "Blink" sketch and choose the button for Arduino Upload (The LED that is on the board of the Arduino will flash as a result of the loaded sketch). The sketch will have to run for you to know that the Arduino software and driver has been successfully installed.

Which Arduino IDE version to choose

The manufacturers of Arduino are constantly improving their product and as a result, there have been frequent modifications in the type of

Arduino IDE that they have been releasing. These modifications are necessary because of the continuous users' need that has been arising.

The oldest version of the Arduino IDE is the version 1.0.5, this is the first-ever released Arduino IDE that has been used for various Arduino programming. In fact, this first version and other versions that were previously released such as versions 1.8.11, 1.8.10, 1.8.9, 1.8.8, 1.0.5, 1.0.4, 1.0.3, 1.0.4,0023, 0022, 0021 0020 etc. are now obsolete.

The last version that was released was version 1.8.12. The latest version of the Arduino IDE is version 1.8.13. The version1.8.13 is the best version that has been made so far because of its many improved features.

This version was updated recently and has support for operating systems used mainly by Windows (like 2000, XP, 7 and Vista). It has a total file capacity of 90.20 MB and is developed by Genericom. Some of the other features of this

Arduino IDE include ability to share details with any other person working on an Arduino based project, ability to alter schematics and internal layout whenever it is necessary.

Arduino IDE online

Another way that can be used for programming with the Arduino is using the Arduino IDE online or the Arduino web editor. This is one of the features of the Arduino create which allows you to access tutorials, configure boards and most importantly write codes directly from online. This is good especially if you have a good internet connection.

The advantage that this offers is that you will not need to disturb yourself by downloading the Arduino software. It also gives you the edge of storing your sketches on the cloud where they are saved for easy access at any point in time. If you want to use this online edition of the Arduino IDE,

- Install the Arduino create plugin by going to https://create.arduino.cc/getting-started in order for you to connect your board
- Log in to your Arduino account by clicking on the Arduino Web editor (You can always create a new account if you do not have any account before)

After you might have logged in, you will notice that the online Arduino IDE environment is very similar to the Arduino software version because you are able to code from an internet-connected device that is compatible. You can simply upload a new file by clicking on the import button that is beside the "new sketch" button. By doing this, you will be able to run your own code.

The first column of the online Arduino IDE allows you to navigate to various options like sketchbook, examples, libraries, serial monitor, and help. The second column will allow you to see the other options from the menu of any chosen item while the third column serves as your programming environment.

If you want to upload your own libraries, just go to "Libraries" and click on the "Library Manager". With this, you will be able to upload any library that has been stored on your computer. The "Help" tab provides you with several guides on any help you may need or challenge you may face in the course of using the Arduino IDE online.

The amount of storage space that is left on your Arduino IDE online can be seen in the "Preference" tab. This tab also assists you in the course of the programming by offering you with several options which can be used to customize the look of your online Arduino IDE such as the color theme or text size. The most used part of the online Arduino IDE is the code area. This is where you will write your code; verify it and then you can upload it on your Arduino board.

CHAPTER SEVEN

SOME OF THE ARDUINO PROJECT THAT YOU CAN ATTEMPT

The Arduino can be used for many projects which may range from something as simple as using your Arduino to control LED lights to a more complex and technical project like using the Arduino to automate several of your home devices. Below are some of the few projects you can attempt using the Arduino

- **Arduino Mega Chess:** You can have a personal digital chessboard if you are a lover of chess. Some of the basic things you will need for this in addition to your Arduino include a 3D printer and TFT LCD touchscreen. You get to make any necessary change that suits you when designing this digital chessboard.

- **Robot Arm that has Controller:** You can have absolute control over your robot using the Arduino UNO board which has been specially designed for this purpose. You will need to get a robot-arm which usage can be enhanced with the 3D printer.

- **Making musical instruments:** Many hobbyists have used the Arduino to make several musical instruments. The Arduino Uno can also be used for this project. You will also need the Pi supply flick charge for this project. After the project has been completed, you just need to tap on it and it will convert your hand waves to music.

- **The RFID reader security access:** Radio frequency identification can be used to access security. This can be done with the additional usage of an Adafruit NFC card which is being used for security access.

- **Small weather display system:** You can also decide to use your Arduino to make a miniature weather display system. This is really a good project especially for beginners. The weather display system will be programmed for it to display the current temperatures in the environment both in Celsius and Fahrenheit unit. An OLED graphic display may be gotten which will serve the function of showing us the weather.

- **Make a Fingerprint scanner for your door:** This project lets you build a scanner that detects your fingerprint and then allow you to enter through the door to you home. The door will only open at the prompt of your fingerprint alone.

- **Make the control panel of a computer:** The things you can do with the control panel include changing screen preference, controlling the volume, launching of app etc. Your Arduino board is the main brain behind this project while you can control the several other aspects of your computer using the USB controllers.

- **Robotic car:** You can use the Arduino in combination with DC motors to make a robotic car. If you want a robot that has good visual, you can go with the 3D printing for the components of the car. You will also get to learn the rudiments of advanced motor control as you do this project.

- **Motorized camera that follows motion:** This project can be a very good replacement for your home security camera. Your home security camera may not be able to take videos of some blind spot. With the motorized camera following motion, you can be sure that your home will be totally secured as the camera will always follow the direction of any movement that it sense.

- **Quality control system for water:** The water quality sensors can be used in combination with the Arduino UNO to make a great water quality control system for you especially if you are really concerned about your water hygiene.

- **Ultrasonic distance finder:** This is another project that can be tried out using the Arduino Uno in combination with a sonic ranging module and LCD readout. It is used to estimate distances. Sonic waves that is reflected off an object is being detected by a receiver, the data received as a result of this this is then used to give an estimate of the distance to the said object.

- **High speed set of photography:** With the Arduino board, you can now take the slow-mo shots of very fast images such as falling water. In this project, the Arduino board is used with the right flash. This is particular good is you are into photography as it enables you to create wonderful production contents.

- **GPS tracker:** A smart GPS tracker can be designed using the Arduino. This tracker can help to track the position of many things including your car. Other things that are need in combination with your Arduino for this project include GPS module, wires, OLED display etc.

- **Alarm-clock radio:** This Arduino project allow you to use your device for two different functions which are as an alarm and as a radio. There is display of time on your project and you will always be alarmed on any desired time of your choice.

- **Plant watering system:** One of the advantages of the plant watering system when compared with some other Arduino projects is that it can be done within a few hours. By using the right source code, layout component and moisture sensor, you can build the automated plant watering system to fit your taste. The potted plants may be growing on your lawn or balcony, it really does not matter where they are growing.

- **Inverter:** Many people are usually amazed that the Arduino can be used as a sort of substitute to the inverter. The average inverter is more costlier when compared with an inverted made from Arduino. To do this, you can just go ahead and buy your battery, then configure your Arduino to take the function of the inverter.

- **Walkie-Talkie:** Arduino, in combination with some other necessary electronic can be used to make a Walkie-Talkie. This makes it easy for you to communicate with any other person within a set frequency. The medium used to enhance this communication is the Bluetooth.

- **Oscilloscope:** The Arduino board and your computer can be used for building an oscilloscope. The Arduino board serves primarily as the signal acquisition hardware. After this oscilloscope has been built, it can read frequency that is up to 5 KHz. This is made possible as a result of the in-built analog/digital converter that comes along with the Arduino board. The signals from this converter are sent via the USB to your computer.

CHAPTER EIGHT

TROUBLESHOOTING SOME ISSUES WITH ARDUINO

Although, the Arduino is generally very easy to use, some users however find it a little bit difficult to operate. This issue can usually be fixed with some little adjustments here and there. Below, we have looked at some common issues you may have with your Arduino, especially if you are a first time user, and how you can fix them

- **Issues with the serial monitor:** Sometimes, you will need to use the IDE serial monitor. The function of this is that you will be able to send some data through the serial port. Aside from this, it has always been used to show the details of a graph sensor data or an RFID tag.

  Problems usually arise when you begin to see some strange characters (sometimes you may not even see anything at all) when you view the serial monitor. This is usually the case when you did not use the right derail settings. This can be fixed by ensuring that the baud rate settings in the set-up code has the same value as the one in the serial monitor

- **Computer/IDE not recognized by the board:** Refusal of the Arduino board to recognize the computer or IDE is the most common issue when it comes to the Arduino set-up. This problem can arise as a result of two things

1. **Using the USB cable:**Sometimes the USB cable you are using may not let the Arduino recognize the computer or IDE. This is because some USB

cables are designed to be used for charging of smartphones instead of to transmit data. It is usually recommended that you use a USB cable that has a very good microcontroller. This will even make programming and powering your device very easy.

2. **Board drivers:** Although board drivers are usually automatically detected by your device. This allows easy automatic installation. In some cases however, the drivers may not be automatically recognized. If this is the case, then, you will need to install the drivers by yourself. These drivers come in different form based on the kind of the Arduino board that you are using.

- **Libraries/Header files missing:** For some codes that are being copied from online and pasted on the Arduino IDE, there is a good chance that the necessary libraries for such codes are not already installed on your device. This often leads to an error-message prompt. To fix this issue, all you have to do is just to install the missing libraries. This can be done by looking for the

Library Manager from your computer or just look for the library online.

- **Inability to upload a code:** The inability to upload a code may be caused by

1. **Not using the correct settings for your board:** If you are programming a board and you are not using the right settings for the Arduino IDE for that board, then you may not be able to upload any code to your Arduino. However, if you are using the correct settings, the code will effortlessly upload.

   To fix this issue, you need to open your Arduino IDE environment and go to the "Tool menus" to find for the type of board you are using. If you cannot find the board type here, then, just go directly to "board manager" to add the type of board you are using to list.

2. **Incorrect code:** The Arduino IDE will constantly alert you if there is any error in your code. You will see this alert at the bottom of the IDE within a black box. This can be fixed by re-writing the correct code. Otherwise, you can

simply turn on the verbose output option for your IDE settings. This will give you better suggestion concerning code uploads and guide you in the course of uploading any code of your choice.

FAQS

Some frequently asked questions and answers about Arduino

Still wondering about some certain things you need answers to? Below, we have tried as much as possible to give the best answers to some frequently asked questions concerning the Arduino

Is the Arduino IDE different from the Arduino web editor (online)?

Answer: The Arduino IDE and the Arduino web editor basically perform the same function which is creating an environment for you to write your code. But while the Arduino IDE will be downloaded on your device before you can use it, the Arduino web editor enables you to do the same thing online without the need for you to download any Arduino software

Which board can I use if I decide to use the Arduino web editor?

Answer: All types of Arduino boards can be used with the Arduino web editor

How do you power an Arduino?

Answer: The type of Arduino board you are using will dictate the exact power requirement you are to use. For instance, a 7-12V power adapter or a 5V USB connection can be used to power an Arduino Uno Rev3.

From where can I get the Arduino?

Answer: Arduino can be bought online from Amazon

How can I connect a LCD with an Arduino?

Answer: The LCD screen is linked with the Arduino by the input/output pins. This screen is controlled by using the Liquid Crystals library. To get started with this, go to the library manager and install it.

Can Arduino control many servo motors?

Answer: A maximum of about 12 servo motors is supported by many Arduino boards. About 48 servo motors are supported by the type of Arduino board known as the Arduino Mega boards.

Does relay work well with Arduino?

Answer: Relays work well with most Arduinos. A relay module is often used to control the relay with your Arduino. The connection is made possible by pins which are on the Arduino. This makes wiring them into a circuit a very easy option.

How do you program using the Arduino?

Answer: The Arduino IDE language is popularly known as Processing. It is in this language that programs are created. After this, some files (called sketches) are used to save these programs. These sketches are then uploaded into the Arduino via connection of the computer and the IDE.

What can I do with my Arduino?

Answer: There are many things that you can use your Arduino for. Basically, the Arduino is used in much hardware to send and interpret signals. This signal makes it easy for the Arduino to communicate with this hardware thereby making it to perform several functions depending on the type of project you are using your Arduino for.

Why is the Arduino IDE showing "uploading sketch" without end?

Answer: Sometimes when you begin to upload a program, it may hang. You can simply click on the upload button again. This will start the process all over again so that you may be sure that the program is uploading. This should not take more than 10 seconds.

Can alternative serial monitors be used with the Arduino?

Answer: Yes, you can use alternative serial monitors with your Arduino. Because your computer is being connected with the Arduino by a USB via a virtual serial port, Arduino will read any application that is on your computer. This is why you are able to write and load programs into your Arduino.

CONCLUSION

Because the Arduino is an open-source tool that can be used by any person at any level, it has been provided easy access for many people to use its platform for the execution of various automated projects. In fact, many embedded engineers have been perfectly using the Arduino to even finalize some of their projects. Hobbyists too have had wonderful experience using this priced device.

The Arduino projects have, over the years, contributed to the way many interactive devices are being made. In fact, many Arduino projects have been made to be the prototype of the real projects. In this way, experimenters will be able to make many necessary adjustments before they create the final product.

Aside from this, the Arduino can be used at home for many simple and complex automation processes. This is because the manufacturers of this board have several varieties of the boards which are used for different functions.

At the Prix Ars Electronica in 2006, the Arduino project was recognized as one of the projects which may revolutionize the way things are done especially when it comes to internet of things (IoT). Recently, the Bett Award for "Further Education or Higher Education Digital Services" was won by the Arduino Engineering Kit.

The major significant thing about the Arduino is that you have total control over what and what not you want the Arduino to perform. This is because your boards will only perform the set of instructions that has been sent. This is especially good for beginners in the world of embedded engineering or interactive objects as they get to build many scientific and engineering instruments whose costs are low.

If you have therefore been considering that which platform outside there may offer you the best when it comes to simple and complex automations, then, the Arduino may be the way for you to go as it offers easy set-up and on-the-job training for the many necessary things you can put in place so that your project become a success. Remember, you can automate your home to your desired taste using the Arduino.